The Book of Changes

ALSO BY MADELINE SONIK

FICTION

Drying the Bones

Arms

Belinda and the Dustbunnys

POETRY

Stone Sightings

NON-FICTION

Afflictions & Departures

ANTHOLOGIES

When I Was a Child: Stories for Grownups and Children

Entering the Landscape

Fresh Blood: New Canadian Gothic Fiction

The Book of Changes

Dev Heah

poems by

Madeline Sonik

*Thanks so much for
coming tonight!*

May 30 2012

inanna poetry & fiction series

Inanna Publications and Education Inc.
Toronto, Canada

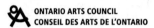

The publisher gratefully acknowledges the support of the Canada Council for the Arts and the Ontario Arts Council for its publishing program.

The publisher is also grateful for the kind support received from an Anonymous Fund at The Calgary Foundation.

Library and Archives Canada Cataloguing in Publication

Sonik, Madeline, 1960-
        The book of changes : poems / Madeline Sonik.

(Inanna poetry & fiction series)
ISBN 978-1-926708-68-3

        I. Title. II. Series: Inanna poetry and fiction series

PS8587.O558B66 2012   C811'.6   C2012-902017-6

Cover design by Valerie Fullard
Printed and bound in Canada

Inanna Publications and Education Inc.
210 Founders College, York University
4700 Keele Street
Toronto, Ontario, Canada M3J 1P3
Telephone: (416) 736-5356 Fax (416) 736-5765
Email: inanna.publications@inanna.ca Website: www.inanna.ca

For my pool pal, Marek

Contents

The Creative

The ladybug's wings spread
on her black back, she cannot see
the eyelash legs of love —

this is how
she creates the world
how the whole world
was created
in a fumble for firm footing,

kernels of red and orange passion
punctuated by the eyes of night
punctuated by dark
clumsy longing.

The Receptive

I taste the treasures
of your apples

words hanging over a fence
sometimes dressed
in green worms
but accepting

I gather those that fall
(stray stones
wriggled from stars
rolled in a raven's beak)

I place them in the pockets
of my ears

warm as earth
I am
full

Difficulty at the Beginning

At first,
it was your mother
a falcon swooping down
calling at 6:00 a.m.
she thought it "evil"
to sleep after dawn and then
our daughter who made me sick
for eight months
before her traumatic birth
you witnessed paralyzed, and still
your mother every sixty seconds
demanding the nurses
let her speak to you, insisting
you couldn't endure.

When we finally took our baby home
she howled like a jackal
for forty-eight hour stretches,
slept for two, the only time
we had, we cried holding
each other sobbing out
the possibility of adoption

and your mother, still
relentless calling and dropping by
carting the baby off
just when she'd fallen asleep.

All those beginnings
have ended; new ones
sharper than trowels
have taken their place
thrusting into the clay
of our marriage
softening
even the hardest edges.

Youthful Folly

In a tacky English seaside hotel
I made friends with the chef
who bitched
complained we weren't moving fast enough
while the plates scorched our fingers
and our sweat rolled into the pork.

Just sixteen
but I stopped walking, turned and roared
"If you can't take the heat, get out of the goddamned kitchen."

I was serious
but he laughed
until he choked, vulnerable
as a red-faced brat.

After that, he gave me things
bought me lager in the pub
told me to call him Uncle,
and I did believing
he cared for me
in an avuncular kind of way.

I loaned him fifty pounds
when he couldn't pay a parking fine
and when his wife was gone
went home with him for dinner.

He cooked us masses of steak and mushrooms,
potatoes and onions, my wine
he doctored
with Rohypnol.

As he was struggling
to unbutton my jeans
I woke
and threw up
in his face.

I saw him in the street
once after that
and thought only
how I'd loaned him fifty pounds
and he'd never paid me back.

Hexagram 5

Waiting/(Nourishment)

You are busy
so I wait

watching clouds of slate
gather in the sky;

there is a darkness in god's eye
the place of light's perpetual dance

and nothing
can be done

before the rain has fallen.

I will stop
and think of you

as raindrops
salt the earth

and residue of joy
ignites the hope
of this rebirth.

Hexagram 6

Conflict

Your blond-haired daughter was at her mother's house
weeping over the bloody divorce;

the squirming issue of your infidelity
still bawled
though you'd left twenty-seven years ago
unfaithfulness stamped its mark upon her face
everything she looked at
was tainted by its expression.

Even love
became a restoration project
and childhood
a place she could never leave:

How could she forgive you?
How could she forsake you?

These twin bars
impossible to uncouple.

The Army

Wars of words
are all
short lived

in the end
there is nothing
to fight over

we move to our corners
open our books
in time all the pages rot

Hexagram 8

Holding Together/Union

Tonight we talked about the future:
if you would sell the house
or live here by yourself
and we noticed
in this talking
how much better we became
how this death
(when we refrain from speaking
in tight-lipped denial)
kills everything around us
just like in our families
when we never mentioned it
(not even when the stink of cancer
stung our eyes.)

Yet here in our house
we allowed the upset
to do its damnedest
to make us weep until

our heads were sore
and, for the crying,
we could breathe again, discovering
in this talking
that no one ever really leaves
they just get closer.

Hexagram 9

The Taming Power of the Small

Out of reach
the safety of seeing you:
heaven draws away —

earth that I am
I sink
alone;

the mulberry
burdened once with flowers of fruit
is also ravaged;

the axe knows only
          endings/
                    separations —
finality that stamps itself
like a wax seal
over brittle leaves
and stains the silkworm's art

roots, still
too bereft
to divine a channel back
through solid clay.

Treading/Conduct

Bridled in a silver row boat
beached at the edge of a corn field

no one knows
why it was abandoned.

Her brother tells her
she shouldn't fear the birds

black crows and swallows
landing on the prow,
she wants to fly away
because she reads their minds:

      it's people
      all people
      their sharp beaks
      sneer

      but they don't envision violence
      eyes pecked, bald heads scarred
      they judge only

how inferior
how mutant and grisly

she wishes she would not hear the way they thought.

Hexagram 11

Peace

Bright star shines silver
Morning spills over mountains
Today's flower blooms.

Standstill (Stagnation)

There in the yard
where I'd envisioned a garden
hyacinth flowers, oregano, clumps of effusive lavender
someone has planted
      a stag.

My daughter's boyfriend?
always the practical joker —
but how did he carry such a load
over scrub and rockery
      pose it
      just so
under brittle Garry Oaks
a fraction to the left of my heavy stone goddess?

I do remember pranks from university:
cars on clock towers,
ransomed bronze cannons and concrete generals
stolen and returned
in daylight
though no one ever saw —

but the boyfriend is an actor
not an engineer
and as I ponder how
those driftwood horns
washed above the rangy mottled mosses
creating this stagnant
effigy,
its nervous ear
swivels, a clock hand
triggered by the neighbour's barking dog:

such a small unequivocal gesture
that forces me to hunt
for blood and entrails;
the frothing white
spittle of madness and disease

because even though hale and strong,
life without
cultivated borders,
without well-embalmed features,

is far too unpredictable
to meet
any other way.

Fellowship with Men

Over beer and guitar chords
that echo through the constellations
of our spines
the liquefaction in flesh
reveals moments melting
sediments, solitudes

Hexagram 14

Possession in Great Measure

What is being built in these pits of earth
these places of yellow clay
and wet concrete?

Workmen old enough to be our grandfathers
whistle and trade us cigarettes
for our smiles
their lighters flickering
as we pretend to inhale their lust
then run from them;

at night when they leave
we chase each other
through the skeletons of houses
by moonlight, play tag

believing these games
childish, knowing
the only fire
worth capturing
is the moon's.

Hexagram 15

Modesty

I wore the dresses
that my mother sewed
full skirts belling
over crinoline —
like flowers

a homely Scarlet
O'Hara
but timid and mute
as a bee.

My grade three teacher
who thought me well brought up
approved my modesty
and called me "honey."

I savoured those nectarous
attentions, regardless
that what she admired
was my self-loathing
folded in the petals
of a pretty dress.

Hexagram 16

Enthusiasm

How she dances
on those rusty pegs
desperate for release
in love
with the dance itself
its vain twirling, its whirlpool
edges, ending
her own impulsive
gyrations.

In the yard
the spruce and sycamore
partner her;
they hold her limits
render free
the play of fingers
where imagined chains of vines
like nightshade
lash the doors and windows
of those who'd halt
her pulsing reel.

Hexagram 17

Following

From the banks of Styx
your boat beating
the bars of my prison

whose pillars paddle
the futile clouds
of heaven; his face
burns fresh always
glowing like the oil
I let spill upon his wings

to brace him
to the earth and me:

calculated action
at husband-catching
I have suffered for,

nothing more
than this longing
to be loved.

You turn your head,
Ferryman, but listen
to the way he left

and how I followed in his stream
of breath
arriving everywhere he passed
too late.

Mothers, I invoked
more tragic than bleating lambs
with orphan
offerings begging
for forgiveness
forbearance, the passe-partout
that might unlock me
from his flesh
turn me forward
in a union
with my self;

my own blackened body
purling like a maple key
pummeled and pitched
from a talking tower
that said I had fallen
into everywhere
that wasn't heaven:

my loveliness
could inspire everyone
but me.

Ferryman, carry this cry
to those echoed pastures
where lutes of love that mar mortal women lie
and scar us with the loss
of wanting
gods.

Hexagram 18

Work on What Has Been Spoiled

worms breeding in bowls
we left our beer unfinished
we could meet again
in dreams or by the ocean

Approach

Coming to him
cold-footed as Mary
blundering in his fecund revelations
of love, buzzards
wait beyond
his wreath of winterweed.
The woman he wears down
bends like a seedling
under the blown-out night.

She would give him
all her power, hold
his hunger
in her leaves
wrap herself in muddy
oblivion so his jaw slack
as twine could trick
the moment longer.
Worms could inch
over her broken
branches in the armour
of a knotted thrust.

Hexagram 20

Contemplation

To make a significant mistake

as in miss take:
what we fail to pick up,
an action completed
poorly, as on a movie set
when the hero and heroine kiss
without chemistry —
"take one, take two…"
or a photograph
where we're frozen
blinking back rage.

Miss Tache:
an unmarried woman from the Balkans
who tried but couldn't stop
the bank's sexist practice
offering more credit than she could afford
on envelopes personalized by honorifics —
reminders that even still
status is attached

to being men's chattel.

mist ache:
a pain
in the mist
or a pain caused by evaporation of …
or the blindness …
like a ship crashing
and sinking in the fog
on a warm day
when we fail to pick up
that we've done something wrong
or he has
and all our attempts
to define
exactly what that was
have ended
in this
pointless, circuitous
charade.

Hexagram 21

Biting Through

Your sister feared
I'd find my heart
in the peeling plywood cupboard
painted white
above the range

in your childhood home
heaving with twists of green ivy
on tattered papered walls —
she stripped the light
to prevent my seeing:

what you savoured,
the morsel I had offered
sweeter and more
blood-red
than any preserve.

Grace

I dreamed about the rancid smell of hay
as if a frightened horse
had mauled it from his mouth
into a tube

something small and narrow
I'd have to crawl through
before they would remove
the malignancy:

damp and ashy quills of anesthetic pulp
clung to my lungs
and in this stuck
breathless panic
although my heart   bolted
my mind forced a calm
bringing the whole of me
blinded and swollen
into this soft manger
of waking air.

Splitting Apart

It is hotter than you could imagine
here where dreams of your frightened
face, your lost desperation
shimmer just beyond
my urgent dialing finger —
I waited all evening
for your call
that never came
suspended somewhere
just over hell's gate,

knowing you have a right to live
to lie solitary under the Sitka Spruce
and feel the stars reflecting flames in your eyes
and me
an obligation to die
a hundred times.

In the darkness of these crawling hours
when no phone rings
I remember the seconds
of your birth

ripping open
for all the world
to rush through

yet that tear
could feel no more tender
than this airless night.

Hexagram 24

Return (The Turning Point)

My tide of light, withdrawn
under the mooning oak

when cottonwoods spilled
oceans from their bows

traveled past
the Okanagan grape

now ready to be wine
in your return

liquor with its summons
pulp and seed

the harvest sweetening on your lips.

Innocence (The Unexpected)

I have become ten years old again
lines smooth, eyes trusting
even the silver in my hair
has turned blond
like that summer
when lake and sun
bleached me into beauty.

Thirty-eight years of life
shed away
in an instant of joy
I marvel
at the mystery of me.

The snake movement
of my moods
the pressure points of pain —
artless childhood lingering
under flesh.

Hexagram 26

The Taming Power of the Great

In my garden
green cobras rise from stars
their saffron heads
crowned with stylish afros;

all summer long they appear,
age
puffed and sage
silver white.

Do they lament
their lifetimes spent
beneath oak canopies
or the fickle balding breeze
that plucks away
their seedy tattered memories?

The Corners of the Mouth (Providing Nourishment)

This night
heady with lacquer and shade
you tug at my hips.

Darkness allows
that uptight bouquet
of glaring poppies
to shut
their filthy eyes
and feel
the soft petals
of scarlet kisses
before they fall.

We pretend
this pull
is a mirage
two thirsty mariners
have dreamed
in their passage

assuaging the tongue

reviving the body
taking and giving
from each

an easy river of fire
we agree to burn
every immoral flower

to burn the letters
to burn delight
to drink often
deeply
at this bright oasis.

Preponderance of the Great

What you mean to me
you may wonder

as these two full buckets
of silence

force my stillness
deep into your river

my feet anchored
by love's weight

the water rising
until I know of

things more important
than breathing.

Hexagram 29

The Abysmal (Water)

My tyrant love
will not release

a spring to quench
this hollow lake

that dries and breaks
in veins of dust

for on another's shoulder brushed
joy's unacknowledged touch.

The Clinging, Fire

What has been buried
like a glass egg
in the soft hold
of mute childhood
detonates
blowing out windows
your parents made impenetrable
bringing down fortresses.

The recycled red convertible
you drive smoulders
with the stinking butt
you bite between your teeth.

You know, in the end, it will probably kill you.

Your mother's cold-eyed resentment
your father's phony smile
all these combustible things
conceal terror
and like a match
ignite.

Hexagram 31

Influence (Wooing)

Professor daddy, give me A's
          bounce me with approval
     hold nothing
   back
                        lavish me
               make the echo   good
               rip through me
               pat my head
               contain my shadow
               build me, build me

                                        up

               meet my sharp mind
               love it
               to the centre of your
                        bull's-eye
               ground me, hold me fixed
               don't ever leave me
               hold me
               smother me bright
               like snow that hurts
               exquisite claustrophobia
                        erase me.

Hexagram 32

Duration

No personal connection
only that I found it on a beach
and discovered
what can be imagined into bone:

death, a person's death, or maybe
some animal murdered

a deer set upon
by German Shepherds
or felled by beach logs
and slick black stones

though just a bone
when I found it
I thought about living
imagined breathing on it
and bringing back to life
whatever left it

and how everything
through its absence

can be storied:
the horrors of a family
disease and war
the lack of every
memory like flesh
off the bone
like bone off the body;

I see into what isn't there
imagine into emptiness
everything
that does not exist
for eternity.

Hexagram 33

Retreat

The longhorn cowfish
dotted with white clover
is beyond the memory
of any prehistoric garden.

It is a cross
between snail
and cod

helicopter
and submarine

a being that could not
decide how
it should blossom
what it should wear.

It twirls its three blunt fins like blades

flirts shamelessly
with gawking strangers

bats and winks its bulbous eyes
yearning for an image of itself;

some man says, "crazy,"
"have you ever seen anything
that looks that crazy?"

The longhorn cowfish
submerges to white stone
chops its way through weed
remains   at the bottom
of its bed
well past   closing

Hexagram 34

The Power of the Great

I lifted a stone from the beach
and it spoke to me
saying: "I am God."
I touched the sand
with the bones of my hands
and it purred like a cat:
"I am God."

In the sky
the clouds configured
"His Majesty," and I called to him;
"I am God," he called back.

And the water
cascaded a voice
into the void
"I am God."

At the convent,
I'd taken precautions
against mirrors;

vanity was a scar
I carried on my face

but it happened
that a round bowl of a silver spoon
fed me a reflection,

"I am God,"
I whispered, frightened
"I am God."

Progress

Comfortable body
it has taken us so long
to fit.

My squirming soul
and your expandable
expendable
pulpy pocket;

I've pushed out
mountains of life
in you, hewn
hollows of grief
torn and toned
willful muscles of delight
raged over our evolving
landscapes, each ridge
ripple a work in progress
taking years to realize
the promise
of a solitary wrinkle.

Hexagram 36

Darkening of the Light

The dark flaring of light
is when the earth is above
fire that cannot burn
a path through your broom
and golden rod
over ocean and stones
to the field
where I am turning
your words
over and over
with my tongue,

a feast by necessity
the lover's silver lips
must clasp down upon,

the rough red match heads
learn to accept their solitary tastes,

externally there is nothing
to mark this ignition

struck across a board
of sand or bark,

what flares in the bowl of the throat
is swallowed and borne
along with small yellow flowers
brown velvet and cotton seed
sulfur and fish roe mutely multiplying.

Hexagram 37

The Family

We sit at pool side
keeping our children
from danger
feeling as inflated
as the orange water wings
our three year old daughter
has learned to trust.

The older one
can swim now
and we are gratified by this
though no one here knows
of long hours
whole summers
spent with her
clinging to our backs
and reassuring words
promising water's magic
just like school and heaven:
"believe in it, and it will sustain you."

It's easy now she's fallen in love

with weightlessness
the endurance of her own
small body's stroke
that no longer needs
strengthening
by pride.

Hexagram 38

Opposition

While I was trying to write
a small dark boy came in
hurling daggers at wooden doors
crushing miniature vials
under playground soil.

In the monkey bars
where obedient, literate children dangled
he took no aesthetic interest.

His eyebrows, diminutive bat wings, arched
his tongue, a purple supine snake
exhibited its belly's contempt
as he smashed the shuddering
innocent frame
felling children like cherries.

He thumbed his ugly nose at me,
his ears sealed
against sweet-talk
and immune to threat
until all concentration spent

I shouted: "What on earth do you want?"

Rubbery lips twitched
past pointed teeth
eyes like origami roses
blazed in victory.

He took one last whack
at the monkey bars
gave me a quick, audacious
highway salute, then dashed
like a solitary hyphen —
right into the poem.

Hexagram 39

Obstruction

white haloed tumor
in this spherical gantry
contained as the breath
I am told
to hold

innards light up visions unuttered
goggle-eyed radiologists prognosticate

celestial complications

Hexagram 40

Deliverance

The mare who hauled me here
sweats wildly
in the fern garden
fuming at my carelessness.

Three years ago
I left her
and let myself
be taken in

let myself
inhale the poison
of a burning lie
thinking I could choke
the flames

and divide my self
in mind
from body;
for thoughts alone
are easy to command —

grand words
smother the gentle neighing
of flesh.

I lost my way
when the ear
of my body
failed to hear
the horse sense
rearing
in my gut, driving its
sick sapience
into pockets of proliferating
cells that knocked
me on my ass
threw me so far
from anything
dishonest
that the noxious ash
blew clear away
right across
an ocean.

I thank her
for her ornery peril
for all the hell
she galloped loose

for all the breath
she's brought me through
knowing my adherence
strong and steady now
to the fix of her flanks.

Hexagram 41

Decrease

What is the yellow sailfin
trying to tell you?

If the water
in its aquarium
did not drown its
flat warm voice

what volcano
of tart words
would it spew

spitting a rubbery bandage
of dark blue fish skin
from its puckered hole?

Would its mouth
erupt the summons
to enter its mind

and swim over
the cerulean scales

it hurls?

For there is no meat

no meat at all
no meat what so ever

in this tight and turquoise silence.

Hexagram 42

Increase

Formed from first
family silences
where she is still netted
haunting my cathedral:
a shadow skinny
adolescent carving
in fine indelible lines
the graffiti of desertion.

There were assaults
that shelled her
almost empty;
still cursives of nerve
dust in its compression
clinging.

She salvaged the mounting words
as if by a mother's
certain fist.

Break-through (Resoluteness)

When a character talks back
it's like taking a needle
and sticking it into a place
where bone and muscles knot
over paragraphs.

Your female specimen,
the woman of your inquiry,
Luna Moth,
responds with a knee jerk
osculation.

All the time
you thought her wings
were made of paper,
that black ink
was a colourless substance
you could use to stain her lips!

Jab more with your pen —
her voice will rear up

so earth-splitting
you'll think it's
a hurricane
shaking safe tiles
from your sound theories.

Coming to Meet

I dreamed of Eros:
his gaunt face
his crystal wings
before he flew away.

I lived to the limit
of my glass tent, wet face
pressed against pain, separating
and sowing seeds, blocked
from his embrace.

The arduous myth
opens a tomb
to fall through
finding him in every man
in the moon
upon the land
extending a hand
desolate, adrift

Hexagram 45

Gathering Together

The finches in the oaks
pop like popcorn
while the hummingbirds
buzz and tick
like clocks.

It's more than
the neighbour's cat
walking through hedgerows
that makes them wake
the camouflage of leaves
and call, evening
absorbing day, the still
blue sky a palimpsest
for raiders of the sea
white as Noah's doves

the finches in oaks
like schools of minnows
confirm light
shadow dive
in feathered tangles
of agitated joy.

Pushing Upward

Look at the world
reflecting jade and fuchsia
in your cheap glass shade —
the perfect dimensions of windowed sun
spreading out like Utah
across a map.

But this isn't a map,
this isn't the world:
it's only a room where you lie
heavy as tired gas
rooted like a tree
with your wrinkled clothes
tossed on posts
teacups teetering
on library books.

You ask what fines you incur
by not growing past this shelter
know that noisy, silly birds
become artists
just like you

their twig edifices and blue eggs
all made without
their knowing. If only
you would wake
shake your spine
free from the feathers
of your primal eiderdown
crashing wind would break
the weak wood of your branches.
The coloured windows
that keep you from grasping light
would open to
the ends of the earth.

Hexagram 47

Oppression (Exhaustion)

I want to be one
accepted,
girls can pack pistols
like men
the roulette wheel spins
red black   red black
and my back
where the knife sticks in;

corset — escort — husband
container of harlots
hold guts,
if I run run run
in a circle
I pretend
I just keep up;

carving the full-bellied
pumpkin
steel in the palm of my hand
making a pie and a face
and my eye

drops like jelly;
the bullet goes in.

The bartender
stands in the corner
his collar the size
of a cunt

         ladies   stay out

and I scream and shout
while he grunts and he grunts
       and he grunts.

The Well

This greedy beast
who with its simple ardent thirst
wants a simple fuck
to lay heaven bare

in supreme stupidity
is blind to the release
of the hordes of helldogs
who devour it.

How did it let the innocence
of its spell spill into hell
when all it sought was God's well
and the quenching relief
of its own burnt tongue?

Revolution (Molting)

Legions of toothed dandelion leaves
pierced and besieged
the garden's
verdant blades

jousting jaundice crowns,
they crushed their bracts
and achenes
into barren
leeways found

insinuating seed over
compliant populations
scattering their progeny

taraxacum

brash and phallic
conquerors.

The Caldron

I was afraid to go in
because I know corrosion's hunger
how bacteria grows
in fetid vessels
jungles and families
where people kill
with words.

A pact turns toxic
comfort is for withholding
blistering blame follows a nerve
in the neck
that stops you from seeing:

the cadmium orange couch
that stinks of your father;
the way your mother's cigarette
smoke stains the jaundiced crippled walls.

There's an arsenal behind family oak

cupboards, cake frosting turns
to napalm while red dead things
served with a maître d's care
roast in a tin bucket.

Hexagram 51

The Arousing (Shock, Thunder)

Your heart against my back
peeling the damp bark
off pink arbutus flesh.

In this charge
we pretend
we are strangers

me thinking of Ontario
thunderstorm streaks
of light purging streets
skipping over lakes

stones, speckled trout,
the rain that turned
to ashes on my lips.

Over the miles
a chair creates between us
I cannot speak

cannot travel past

the threshold of your eyes
the lake's lightning I miss
most; muddy green,
churning in my chest
flashing cobalt

mirrors reflecting
everything
my body feels

naked and immodest
as a water lily
splayed afloat
upon the mire

love that must be left
to grow like rushes
in a sewer
after rain.

Keeping Still, Mountain

at the base of this snow washed mountain
rising steep to heaven

the spade of my tongue
still longing

to rest
in the land-light of your lips

between patient obsession
the pulse continues

measuring illuminations
of desire

with motion ending
the perpetual wish

Hexagram 53

Development (Gradual Process)

In time
kaleidoscope
illuminations on the way
station to decay
form bright blue stars,
emerald flowers

while shards of broken
tortured glass
replace our eyes.

Attachment is in
holding that the mirrors
we've composed
must never break —
that breaking
reflects the end
and not the apotheosis
of shifting light.

Hexagram 54

The Marrying Maiden

You walk through shade
imaging these fanning arbutus
stretching over your life
your wife, at home,
making dinner.

For twenty years
you've known the scents
of her moods
when to touch her
when not
to say hello.

Her eyes were the great mysteries
you entered into

tides and ocean tunnels
chanting and changing
turning nuances of aqua blue

but now it is you

this home and hearth
this hot tea
this soft bed
you sink in.

Have you always wanted
more?

"Why is it men can't have several women
and women several men?"

It is a conversation
she will not allow
you even
with yourself:

this Christian woman
who believes in the trinity
of one

a heavy burden
for any man

Hexagram 55

Abundance/Fullness

Let the great years
when you were leader
fold like the slow beating wings
of a heron
and stop you
from looking back
at all that wreckage.

The Wanderer

Because everything I wish for is impossible, because I am in Active Pass, with windy waters rattling china cups, because the cover of your city's luster has folded behind me and I can no longer see your light. I will search for you here, sparking voluble seeds, behind this dark glass.

      You say the ocean makes phantoms of all who wander, who grow from trees and leaves to heaven, who drive these crossings with the tired oars of their fists.

      You say we cannot hold the salt above the water, nor the air above the earth, and so we must surrender to time and flesh, angelfish in their antipodean dance with slick and spiraling currents.

      You say there are always two in every reflection.
Two worlds to navigate, two
        incongruous shores:
what is possible, what is impossible
what is passing, what must come to pass.

Hexagram 57

Sun/The Gentle (The Penetrating, Wind)

You have dispersed these clouds
gathered this darkness from my sky
revived the sun,

in your gentle deception
your transparent prints
stroke and penetrate stone,

just a shaft
of your warmth
allows my melting

wet and light
pooling
into the palms of your hands.

The Joyous Lake

Blood-red
thorn rose
into my dreaming fingers—

your pulse
the pulse of the rain
thrashes through my hands.

I send my prayers to her
and watch them carry
over wet branches

of rowan, love,
to your door
in morning

like milk and bread
from a truck, love,
beating a channel

through breath;

spirits converge

small glistening red berries
steam rising from pavement, from flesh,
racing to meet you.

Hexagram 59

Dispersion

Fast red ball bounces
over the highway to fields
the girl chases this
sun rolling farther from her
sun rolling farther away

Hexagram 60

Limitation

I dreamed
the front yard
flooded with lilies
and pond water
threatening to rot
the house I live in.

Just too much
proliferation
wildly teeming
dirt and life
that didn't belong
in this space
and must be torn from the roots
pumped clean
stripped away;

burgeoning flowers
without restraint
that must never know
the welling hope
of a warm season
or a second coming.

Hexagram 61

Inner Truth

On my way
to dying
I see messages everywhere:

"Let the Energy Save You"
shouts an ad
from the back of a bus;

I wonder
what this energy is:

maybe the baby
I didn't want
and refused to carry
in my dreams.

Thinking over this paradox:
how life is only possible
in death's reception.

Hexagram 62

Preponderance of the Small

Because you do not
covet the sun

nor command wings
to take you there

the dense earth soft
with clay angels

is high enough
for you are exceptional:

flame, you lift
what is lowly, like me

into the marsh-light
of your hands

press it
to your lips

to love
what is low

is to bless
all life.

After Completion

She perches a broken branch again and again
her toes touch the air —
in this Crow endeavors
to hold the world
to stop
its spilling

its spilling
to stop
to hold the world
in this Crow endeavors
her toes touch the air —
she perches a broken branch again and again

Hexagram 64

Before Completion

The rainmaker meditates in her hut
not beseeching clouds
to wring their drops
over parched plains
but rather with a mind
to align the microcosm
of her moods.

A spine in which
each vertebrae assembles
and reaches snake-like
for a small heat
to fuse the cosmic centre
of her many
liquid selves.

Acknowledgements

I wish to thank Eric Henderson for his critical eye and thoughtful comments and Helen Kuk for her many invaluable substantive suggestions.

Thanks also to George McWhirter, his teachings and his book groups, Carl Leggo, Renee Norman, and the many other dedicated and wise poets and teachers I met at the University of British Columbia.

Many of these poems first appeared in magazines including *Room, Canadian Woman Studies, The Antigonish Review,* and *The Dalhousie Review.* Thanks to these publications and their editors for providing a literary forum for new and budding works.

Thanks also to the spirit of the *I Ching* and the Richard Wilhelm Translation, rendered into English by Cary F. Baynes and published by Princeton University Press, which I consulted in the creation of this collection.

Photo: Claudia Molina

Madeline Sonik is an eclectic, award-winning writer and anthologist whose fiction, poetry and creative non-fiction have appeared in literary journals internationally. Her published book-length works include a novel, *Arms,* a collection of short fiction, *Drying the Bones*; a children's novel, *Belinda and the Dustbunnys*; a poetry collection, *Stone Sightings*; and a collection of personal essays, *Afflictions & Departures*, a finalist for the 2012 Charles Taylor Prize for Literary Non-Fiction. She is also the co-editor of three anthologies: *Fresh Blood: New Canadian Gothic Fiction; Entering the Landscape*; and *When I Was a Child: Stories for Grownups and Children*. She currently teaches at the University of Victoria in British Columbia.